Transitions

A TREATISE **ON**

DEATH AND DYING

BY
VIVIAN GAINES TANNER PAXTON

to the Franck family

Vivian Gaines Tanner Paxton

Special love to Stan

Published by:
Garden Of Eden Press
1- 800 568 3595

Printed in the U.S.A.
Edited by John T. Paxton
ISBN 0-9665755-0-4

I dedicate TRANSITIONS to both Betty White and Lynette Mack, two people whose friendship I will always cherish.

Betty White, a woman I love in death as much, if not more than, as in life. Most people did not know how close our relationship was. She was what I call real kin folk. I could talk to her about anything and even though Betty did not always understand, she never made it a problem. Betty just accepted what I had to say. Oh, she knew I was different! In her own way, she was fascinated by the unusual experiences I discussed with her.

In those days, the beauty shop was in my home and I was Betty's hairdresser. I always made dinner for her when she came to get her hair done, knowing she did not have time to cook. Betty's life was caught up in civic duties. How she loved my Kosher chicken soup with matzo balls, made with fresh chicken feet. She loved my Italian pasta sauces, the southern fried chicken and my West Indian peas and rice. She loved them all and I loved feeding her, although I know we both had to watch our weight.

Betty wasn't one to show feelings outwardly, but they were written all over her. She gave so much to everyone, not asking for anything in return. Her life was meant to benefit others. With her energy she smothered all, to her, sisters and brothers. She received respect and admiration from all who knew her. How I loved that gal!

What surprised me most was that when Betty died, she came to me to let me know it was all so beautiful.

> In her new found life
> No misery, no strife
> But a new way to aid
> Getting ready for her fantastic parade.

Several months later, she came to me in her beautiful white dress and golden crown and showed me that I must lose weight. I paid attention at that moment, then lost sight of what I was supposed to do. It cost me a little suffering. Time passed, and then one night, Betty came to me again. She placed a blue ribbon on my blouse. I said to my husband"Now why did she do that?" Three months later, it was explained. I was notified that I had won the County Executive's Individual Artist Award, administered by the Dutchess County Arts Council, a most selective and prestigious award. There was no other explanation. Betty had broken the bonds of the heaven world to let me know she could help me verify that she is an angel. The last time I saw Betty White, she held a bouquet of white flowers in her hands. She gave me five, one at a time. I have no idea what it means, but in due time, it will reveal itself.

Now you know why I had to dedicate this book to Betty White, so that all who knew her or heard of her will remember this wonderful dedicated woman. We love you, Betty. Carry on your good work. That's why you had to become an angel.

> Your life in the heaven world
> Completely sublime
> Ending just in time
> To take your place
> In the beautiful heaven world
> Filled with grace
> Your life more than anyone will know
> Was evenly paced.

Every time my friend, Doris, came to get her hair done, accompanied by her husband, was a dread for me. I could not understand why this man annoyed me, made me feel uneasy.

Later, I came to know it was because he was dying. I remembered this happening before. When people came around or when they wanted a portrait of their loved one and I couldn't do it, I was sensing something. At the time, I wasn't really sure but I knew something was wrong. Later, when the person was either sick or dying, I came to know why. I especially have good memories of the Mack who used to say to me," Now Vivian, you must sign those paintings ". He was there when I first started painting. In fact, he bought one of my first oils. I'll never forget it. It was a seascape. Mack had once been in the Navy. He loved the water.

He used to tell me my paintings would be worth something someday. I would laugh. Little did I know Mack was foreseeing the future. My paintings are selling and my reputation has skyrocketed enough to make me the recipient of many prestigious awards for contributions to art and community. Isn't that something! I never did know how to gloat about anything, but always a thanks to the Divine source that allowed me to achieve gifts I never imagined possible.

Getting back to Mack, well he asked me to write a beauty hints column for the Mid Hudson Herald, a black newspaper. Well, I told Mack, " You know I don't have the expertise for that ". He insisted I give it a try. I did and it worked out well. There I was, month after month, writing the column for the newspaper. Next, I was doing a little reporting, getting stories and articles about happenings in the

Black community. I really surprised myself and I guess everyone else.

At the time, I owned a beauty shop, did the hairdressing and came in contact with the most interesting people. Those were my stories. These were the people who supplied the information to report, their vacations, their birthdays, parties and social happenings. Was it ever fun until one day I felt pooped out and stopped.

I have wonderful memories of Mack and how he encouraged me.

After he passed away, he came to me to let me know how beautiful it is on the other side of life. I dedicate the treatise to Mack who encouraged me, who felt I had a talent I wasn't aware of. I salute you, Mack. Today, his wife, Doris and I are still friends on earth while he's enjoying his heavenly home.

Transitions

(A Treatise On Death and Dying)

This treatise on death and dying is based on my most unusual and gratifying experience of the other worlds in the after life. It is brought to you with a sincere belief and explicit faith that death is not the end. There are many who will disbelieve, but many more have had their own personal experience of some kind bearing on the para-normal. I am happy to say that the people who will understand and accept this knowledge are in the majority. The others, maybe something will awaken within to replace their skepticism.

I tell my story as I've seen it, nothing added, nothing left out with the exception that it is impossible to describe the magnificent beauty in all its vast detail when one reaches the higher regions of the heaven world.

Reaching the higher regions of the heaven world is worth trying to earn even though these regions are not easily reached. We have free will; it's up to us. Now shall we get on with the transitions.

It's just amazing to think about it, the privilege of being able to see into the heaven world and to watch people make the transition from life to death; from this world to the next world. Some would say Vivian's imagination has gone really wild, but, God and I know better than that. After all this truly Divine gift comes directly from the God source.

I have always been fascinated by this divine gift, mostly because no two people cross the threshold exactly alike. Offering more proof, my imagination does not stretch quite that far, and actually I don't have to prove a thing; but I do want to tell my story in all its glory; the splendor, the beauty, the unusual happenings when one makes the transition from this world to the next world.

I shall commence by writing as one would case histories, not using the real name, although there is no reason,, as most deaths are exceedingly beautiful when the actual transition takes place, no matter how the earthly death might occur. Even so, the souls and the families of the deceased have a right to privacy.

I have watched folks that were dear to me; folks that I knew and folks that I did not know but somehow wanted or allowed me to see their transition. It's just amazing. This special vision has gone on now for quite a few years. It's now time to share as there are so many folks that care. It would stop a lot of grieving and also a lot of misconceiving.
There are times when conversation takes place; now don't start thinking that I hear voices. I don't. I leave that to people who are not themselves, because

there is no such thing as hearing voices unless it's your own voice. With me it's a form of telepathy. I just seem to know, sometimes it's with a sign language. If I ever heard a voice I would take myself to the nearest psychiatrist. Now to get back to what's really important, this amazing transition.

Before I get too deeply involved with transitions, I must share with you another experience that to this very day leaves me mystified. Whenever a person consults me about a particular problem that is something of real import a poem will come into my consciousness, a poem of help, an answer if you will. Well after awhile poems would come to me to comfort the deceased's loved ones. What is so amazing about these communications is that the recipient of the poem would say to me, you could not possibly have known that, or it might be like the deceased was dictating the poem, things they should or should not do, always in a positive vain; always to appease or to please. Such a beautiful thing, how did I ever deserve this privilege, to be of help, to console? All my life I have found it easy to love all. I am so happy to be an instrument of help. The Divine source is so much more powerful than man can imagine, capable of everything imaginable. Miracles do happen, you know, and this beatific vision is indeed a miracle, a miracle I must share. I do care. Love is all.

We all must love all, that's the key, a brotherhood if you will. Changes are taking place, look around, think,, listen, you'll notice. The world is without end you know, destruction here, destruction there, but the world, the earth will exist.

Raise your consciousness up high, reach beyond the sky, answers will abound; life will take on new meaning, clear and sound.

I would like to start with the most recent transitions, then go back to the beginning.

We sit and mourn, we sometimes scorn, we cry, we almost die while the souls are so happy in their new found state. I think of the times when I've heard ministers, priests and other clergymen unable to adequately express the deaths situation. They did not know what to say to a family on the verge of disaster unable to cope with the situation because of guilt feelings when actually there was no guilt; finding ways to blame themselves when there was no blame. Thinking of how they could have done better by their loved ones when they were really doing their best not realizing that their dearly departed are Gods guest. I don't want to get ahead of my story. I must leave the explanations concerning death until the end of my story.

Prepare because I'm going to take you through some of the most amazing situations you ever thought you need listen to; and you must listen because we all have to face the death of a loved one and also have the experience of death ourselves. It is truly an experience we cannot escape and when you read how beautiful it is, this death trip; it will wipe away all fears, at least lessen them; and when your time comes you just might welcome death with the splendor and the glory we are originally led to believe, whatever religious belief.

4

People pray, they say they believe, they have faith, but belief is sometimes very shallow. It takes a lot of deep down thought to really understand and believe in the true power that your God can do anything and your God can, not necessarily grant you your wish. Have you ever wanted something badly; prayed for it and it was not granted and you found out later that the Divine knew best; that the wish would not have been as beneficial as you suspected it would be.

Do you know that when we're born into the world we're given an Angel to guide us. We also have a right to free choice. Have you noticed that when you follow your first impulse, it's always the right choice. That's your Angel's guiding force, when you change your mind that is your free choice.

I realize that with writing this book, my thought goes from one thought to another, well that's my Angel's guidance. I've learned to listen and hopefully take the proper advice. Remember it's all a subconscious happening. The God source is truly wonderful, like no other, it's out of this world.

I remember going for a ride in the country one afternoon feeling quite peaceful, it was a beautiful day. Suddenly I had the impulse to go home. I might have felt a little tired, upon arriving home, I immediately went upstairs to bed; no sooner than I hit the bed, I found myself going through this dark tunnel. Mind you, I know I was not asleep, absolutely not; I was fully awake in a relaxed state. There I was in my soul meeting up with my friends son who was a patient at the local hospital; we walked together down the long tunnel, in the distant you could see the beautiful light. He entered the light. I got right up, went downstairs to tell my husband of this unusual adventure. After awhile the phone rang, I was being informed of the young man's death. Of course, it was of no surprise to me; after all did I not go with him to the entrance into the heaven world.

I was most anxious to speak to his mother, to let her know how beautiful was his transition from this world to the world of the after life, the heaven world. She was reluctant to believe and probably does not to this day. You see, her religion was so against everything so she had a lot of preconceived notions about heaven and who might enter the holy gate.

One thing for sure, I was with him when he made the transit at the exact time he was in the hospital dying; they themselves verified that. He entered in peace and a few days later he came to me for a farewell; I knew that I would never see him again.

A theatrical person was dying a slow death with the dreaded disease called cancer. Every one around was feeling the gloom that comes with impending death. She was a very well loved individual; finally, after much suffering, she passed on. I had the amazing opportunity to watch her make the transition into the heaven world. It was so beautiful. There she was, dressed as a nun gliding up to heaven so gracefully, surrounded by a host of Angels. She really welcomed the heavens as they just seemed to open to her; beaming, her face gleaming, how beautiful. If only her loved ones could see this most magnificent ascent into the heaven world; but they can't so they'll mourn until the day when their time comes and they reach that beatific state. Heaven is for all.

An automobile accident on the North road near an Institute of learning, I could hear folks saying how tragic. She was so young and leaving behind a family. Somehow survivors manage to survive and tragic deaths in my observation, always mean instant heaven. Well it was the first time I had ever seen a soul being escorted into the heaven world by a Jesus figure. She was going so fast, the Jesus figure put His arm out to slow her down and she entered a higher heaven, the Angelic realm with full grace granted. How sweet it was, a magnificent transition.

My dear friend passed away a few weeks ago, we loved her dearly. My son was very upset; she was so good to him, always baking him goodies; no one made chocolate cakes like Aunt Louise. We just felt too close to call her by her surname. What can I say, she was like having another mother, and I really felt privileged to watch her make the transition from this life to the next in such splendor and glory.

When I saw Aunt Louise, she was skipping through a field of beautiful wild flowers, she was radiant, beaming all over with a smile like I had never witnessed in real life. She skipped along, a woman who in real life was so arthritic, she had to sometimes walk with a cane. Through the means of telepathy, she conveyed to me that she had no idea that heaven was quite this beautiful.

That night when I was sitting on my bed, Aunt Louise came to me. This time she was all aglow like in a field of light, in her hand she held a golden crown. I wondered why she held the crown in her hand. Well low and behold, she placed the golden crown on my head; cupped my face in her hands and kissed me on each cheek, then said to me through telepathy, now you be a good girl; everything will be alright. It's all on the way for you. At that moment, I was engulfed with a most beautiful feeling. Then Aunt Louise moved off into the distance, I immediately knew her soul was special and that the only way we would meet up again would be for a special reason. She revealed to me before parting that she had work to do.

The very next afternoon, Aunt Louise came to me and revealed her presence in glowing robes of splendor. A glorious sight with a golden crown on her head, a staff in her hand, into my consciousness was revealed that she was one of the one hundred and forty four thousand to reign in the heavens with Christ. How glorious, what a privilege granted to me.

What a wonderful way to go. Quickly, straight up like a rocket entering the heaven world with such speed; that's the way I saw a local dentist make his transition. A most marvelous man when he was on earth. I had heard of his wondrous deeds and good fellowship with all races. It was so beautiful, if only I could tell.

Not so with another local shoe store owner. He was earth bound struggling to get through the dross, but at last, he was free, on to victory; his battle he had won, son of a gun. You see there's hope for all. No complete fall, an angel will assist as long as you don't resist. Heaven is for all.

A celebrated author had left this world, she did not get far, she was bound to this earth. A singer of religious songs sung all over the world, bound to the earth, struggling to get free; deaths sting but where is the victory. Both were given another chance to advance their soul. Now in heaven, they wait to be given a new mold, the next earthly life.

She lay in her bed in a coma for many years, folks shed many tears. But a glorious existence she had found. She was not really earth bound, half in heaven, half on earth waiting for her new birth.

I saw this young lady long before she had made her transit into the heaven world; but I could not tell, her life was not hell, she was skipping through fields of clover, while nuns watched over her; so gloriously happy. None could understand she was existing on earth in a hospital bed while her soul was in the promise land.
Upon her demise, when the silver cord was broken, her soul did soar high up past the sky on to the Angelic realm.

A man of the cloth was so well respected, he preached in his church week after week, but when he made his transit, heaven he could not reach.

I was amazed, there I was in my soul body
leading this minister, of all people, toward the light.
He did not know how to get to the heaven world.
Mind you, I was not in a trance, nor was I asleep.
My husband was in his bed and I was describing the
event, how I held the minister's hand and escorted
him to the heaven world to the light.

Now in this same town was a young fellow
with a somewhat shady character. Well, I've never
witnessed a transition so beautiful. He was dressed
in royal robes, a beautiful crown of gold and
diamonds on his head, adorned like a saint. Now tell
me who can judge, tell me who can judge, only God
knows the soul. You see now why I tell you what a
privilege to be given a gift of such magnitude;
ordinary Vivian being able to see into man's soul .
Unbelievable! This young man who most folks
would believe to be hell bound, adorned like a saint
making a most holy exit from this life that knew
nothing but sorrow and tragedy for him. God is all
powerful.

A very dear relative of mine was in a state of
nothingness for a long time. I saw him in barren
land, yet this land was not without light. In real life
this relative was believed to be an atheist. I don't
believe there is any such thing. The belief might not
be in the Christian God but there is belief in
something. I was so relieved when he finished his
state of purgatory for want of a better way to say it.
He then went on to a better existence. All is never
lost. The good outweighs the bad, most transits are
so beautiful. With my dear one a score had to be
settled.

10

On earth she was so lovely, everyone adored this young lady. Her earthly end was so tragic. Her family will not forget as she left the world at the hand of another loved one, her own flesh and blood. Today he is no longer confined. We must not judge, it was her time and the way she was supposed to go.

I remember one day she came to visit me (in real life). I saw into her soul. I don't ask, I don't wish these things, they are just revealed to me. I neither bring it on or can I make it go away. When I saw into this young lady's soul, I knew at that very moment that her soul was superior. Her so called untimely death made an impact on the whole town. She has come to me many times since her transit, always radiant. I remember the first time she was adorned as a bride waiting for Christ.

The next day following her demise, a poem came into my consciousness, I immediately gave it to the family; it brought them consolation. They had someone read it at the funeral. I only ask when I share these lovely poems that come from the Divine source that the parties don't reveal my name. I want to share. I really do care. The true source is God, never forget that. The true source is God.

The Angels came to guide her into the promise land. Even though
her exit was tragic to the heaven world, it was grand; for she was
truly an angel. They long awaited the day, when she would leave
her earthly home and enter heaven to stay.
Try not to mourn for her. It's a state of bliss.

Although to us still on earth, we will surely miss her beautiful smile, her gentle ways. She always knew how to make your day. Love and compassion, she did know. We sure are sorry to see her go. Our loss is heaven's gain.

There was an accident near the vicinity of the children's home. A tragic accident resulting in the death of a well respected local woman. Little did I know this woman would appear to me in an inner vision as I was seated in my living room with my family watching television. I was quite taken back by this experience. Why here was this woman standing before me in a beautiful satin dress, silver slippers on her feet and just beaming all over for all she was worth. You've heard that expression (one smile is worth a thousand words), well believe me, her smile was ecstatic.

I told my husband who just ignored me. Later I was to find out that my sharing with him these most unusual experiences were frightening him. I really had no one else to share with at the time. This person came to me many times trying to convey bits of information concerning her transit; and that she would be born again in an earthly body. It's experiences like this that allowed me to believe in more than one earthly life.

Two years later, I was able to share the experience with her daughter who told me she understood, believed and was thankful that I came forth. She felt I should have told her sooner. But how does one know how this type of information will be received.

There are so many out there exploiting in the name of God, making mockery out of wondrous situations, using them for financial gain. Always with the excuse they have to live. Anything that comes from the Divine source to help others must be given freely, as it is given freely to you. After all, is that not the cause of so much unrest today; everything is for material gain. All I can say is wake up. We still have time.

My first experience of seeing people who had made the transit into the after life came quite a few years ago. At that time, I was able to hold an object in my hand or to my forehead and trace it to its origin or see a scene someplace the object had been. To me this was quite a feat. I'm not going to get into that story although I've already written about it a few years back. Somehow the events of last week, the astronauts, and my dear friend and my friend's mother triggered the idea that the time is right; go and tell your story. Let folks know how grand the death situations; that it is not really a death but a relinquishing of an earthly body transiting on to another existence; and even though no two people make the transit in the same way, there is hope for all.

Getting on with my story, I happened to be in my sister-in-laws house that day. I wanted to show her my new found feat. I took her father's watch fob and immediately saw my deceased father-in-law at his favorite pastime, fishing. I described a place in Pleasant Valley where he used to fish. I described his outfit, right down to the high boots he wore; the surrounding landscape that she was very familiar with, I certainly wasn't. She was in awe because this place was so familiar to her. The children were making noise so I walked into the small bedroom and started to hold the object; this time I saw her Aunt who had gone on to the heaven world. She was unbelievably real; as though she were right before me. Her eyes were cloudy like they used to be in real life. She wore a cameo broach she treasured. I told my sister-in-law. She was just amazed, she knew of the cameo broach, she knew that all I told her was true. What she did not know was that I was so very frightened by this experience.

It's a strange thing about people when they have gone on to the life of the soul. They always show you something that can be verified by those living in the earthly world. My sister-in-law knew of the broach, she knew it was all real and not my imagination going wild.

I went around frightened for about two weeks. I prayed that it would never happen again. I just didn't know how I could tolerate this type of experience, but how does one make it go away? You don't, you live with it and you begin to understand it. Then it becomes part of your life. I have already spent half of my life indulging in fears, fears were my God ever since I can remember. Afraid of the dark, afraid of animals, people, you name it; if it was anything to fear I was captured by it. You can imagine the misery, the torture I sustained at the hands of my own fearful nature. Fortunately for me, when the time arrived for me to see into the after life, I had met a woman who helped to lessen my fears and now I welcome seeing people make the transit.

Besides I have no control over this special vision. Like I said, I never wanted to see anyone, not in this world. Later I came to revere this special gift.

It's just uncanny how one can see with such clarity. The way I see is more clear, more real than real. Seeing with the eyes of the soul is like no other seeing.

I remember reading a book written by Rudolph Steiner which said and I quote, "There would be people who would be able to see with the eyes of the soul with such clarity and I hope they would not be mistaken for people deranged and get locked up in a mental institution." I want you to know I'm doing well living in my own home; working at my art and part time hair dressing business and very active in community affairs, especially things geared toward helping less fortunate children. The spiritual part of my life has been very low keyed, mostly because I had to understand the whole situation myself before I could share these experiences with others. After all, some of my predecessors have made my job difficult, what with this occult revolution, the money making schemes, the fakery. I know that by the time my book reaches the press, I will have the proof that my source is none other than the one true living God.

People are continually trying to figure out life and death situations. Why are we here, where are we going, what is the complete function of the brain and the truth about evolution? If we're only using a small portion of the brain, what are its other functions. Why are some people slow while others are supposedly genius? What do we know about the soul, the true source of knowledge? All that is now, ever was and will be is rooted in the soul. The source few have access to. Why, because we've allowed ourselves to become steeped in materialism. Man is his own downfall. We're allowing ourselves to suffer, WE'RE CHAFING AT THE BIT SO TO SPEAK.

There is an answer tried and true, long over due, tw'll put things to rights, lessen our plights. Love of course is the answer. It gives us a beginning, next thing we're winning life's treasures from the tree, the tree of life, the soul source. When man can tap the soul source he'll cure many a disease such as epilepsy and other types of related diseases, mental disorders, yes mental disorders. When we learn to awaken the soul, dormant powers will arise and be a salvation to man. Man was meant to fulfill many a function. He has yet to begin. Raise your consciousness up high, beyond the sky then you will receive and know why. Life will take on new meaning. When you've discovered the source, no more leaning, all will come from the God force.

I had a friend who's sister died in a mental hospital. She was very upset as to the state of her sister's soul. Well, when a person is in distress, I am somehow immediately able to tune into this reservoir of information and come up with an answer. She was relieved to know her sister wore the usual white garment only privileged souls have access to. Her sister was extremely happy to rid herself of the miserable earthly existence. If it were possible to come back, no one would want to leave this perfect life of the soul once the transition is completed; once the person has reached the final stage.

My neighbor had a child who was handicapped. Her whole life was one of confinements in hospitals. When she was at home, she was blessed with a wonderful sister and brothers who attended her every need. The parents were also exceptional people. God had a way of taking care of his own as she was surely an angel. Upon her passing, I saw her dressed as the Infant of Prague (statue in the Catholic church depicting the baby Jesus), her transition was beautiful. I know they didn't really understand when I shared the experience with them, but she was not the type to balk at it either. Such a devoted family, a real role model for others.

I can go on and on and I will, I will. These magnanimous experiences are as overwhelming as they are delightful, filling me with feelings so hard to express. As I am writing today, I'm just amazed beyond this world, the splendor, the magnificence of the landscapes, the beauty of the dominate flowers. It's no wonder that in my own art work, flowers and landscapes are what I'm all about; representing God, yes, representing the Divine in all things.

When I awaken in the morning and before retiring at night, I look out the window to feast in Gods delight and the wonderful landscapes filled with Gods light. Yes light for me, as everywhere my eyes can feast is bathed in beautiful luminous light, the rainbow promised by God. I glory in the brilliant sunsets, I marvel at the dew sparkling like diamonds on the grass in the early morning sunrise. The world is so beautiful, the earthly world that is. The heaven world is more beautiful. We must wait our time to explore this beauty, to receive heaven, paradise is not just for the earth. There's no getting around the fact that we miss our loved ones, but with the right understanding, it's more a sweet sorrow than a pure misery. Isn't it good to know that most do not suffer; and for those that do there is always an angel to assist. All is never lost.

We must not rush our time. We must only be ready so that when our time comes we might exit in. a more glorious fashion. You want to know more, well on with other case histories. There are many.

A few years ago, I used to enjoy a program of the most unusual order, a television program dealing with the unknown, a little bizarre, superstition and the unknown after world. Some of the programs were based on old custom religions and otherwise. I kind of wondered what this man was all about to be able to put together this type of program. If he had personal experiences, or true research. Well anyway, when the man made his transition he was as amazed as I was. Why, here was this man who wrote with such a knowing and yet he did not know or did he believe, but his soul was pure. He wore his white robe, white robes are not for all immediately. This particular man was standing on a hillside looking over to the other side with amazement, because there on the other side was the most beautiful gold domed building; bathed in the most brilliant sun you could ever feast your eyes upon. He stood there with his arms stretched out ready for his entrance into the heavens. Talk about a trip, amazing!

I must continually explain that when I'm in another dimension, the landscapes take on another kind of beauty, unimaginable. A more refined beauty, everything is so clear and pure. Nothing to mar the natural beauty that another dimension possesses. There are no words to really describe the purity of sight or the marvelous feelings that engulf me as I view the sights. I try in my own puny way to describe these wonders. I'm trying, I must inform, you have a right to know. If I'm suffering from some strange malady, let it go on forever and ever. The life of the soul can be so beautiful and even for those who have to wait in their own little purgatory, waiting for an angel to assist them; the waiting will be worth while; as the paradise they will behold is well worth it. The waiting period, the purifying state, all is never lost no matter the earthly deeds. We cannot judge, we must not judge, no we must not judge. We must love, we must believe in the creative force; God by any other name is still God. That spark in all that only has to be lighted; then the flame, and next enlightenment.

I have a neighbor who is also a very dear friend. Her mother in-law was seated under the dryer in my beauty shop. She seemed a bit disturbed. Upon questioning her she told me of her son who lived in another country and was ailing. Of course I sympathized with her, left the room to make her tea and a poem came into my consciousness. A poem as though the woman's son was dictating the poem. The poem explained about his health and that he didn't expect to live long and how she should accept his passing. I was quite surprised. I knew I could not share the poem just yet as it would only worry her more. I did tell her other son, in fact, I gave him a copy. After he made the transition, I gave her the poem, framed; it made her very happy. The contents had a wonderful message to her, an explanation of why. I knew she would read it over and over and each time, it would take on a new meaning.

I knew a lady who had a daughter who was a supposed suicide. After the transition, the daughter appeared to me informing me her death was not in vain. I really had no idea what she meant, her mother knew. I did not pry, as long as she understood and was satisfied. When I told her I was happy.

A lovely lady, so filled with life, quite a zest for living, wanting to do just everything; had planned on building her own little empire for her and her family. A very domineering kind of person, she was always stressing ways to get ahead, reprimanding others for standing still; always quick to admire those able to take the bull by the horn so to speak. Constantly searching for new ways to promote wealth, a very nice person in spite of her aggressiveness. A very nice person, suddenly taken ill, passed over after not too long an illness. When this lovely lady walked up those golden stairs, when she reached her heaven, she was beaming all over. The lady knew what all her searching was about. It was about heaven, the treasures of heaven. Her aggressiveness was not for earthly treasures but the wealth of the true kingdom. It took the transition to show her the realization. Her pot of gold at the end of the rainbow. What a beautiful transition, what a way to go.

I happened to tune into her funeral. I saw her giving a rose to each one of her children. When she came to her husband, he received a white carnation. I knew right then and there his time would come shortly and it did. Two souls blended together as one. The transition was wonderful. How sweet it is, if you could only know; and you will, we all will.

My dear friend Sarah was a quiet unassuming sort of person, went about life without too much enthusiasm. Taking everything in its stride, not given to much worrying; hardly complained. Sarah did the best she could, she was an avid reader, always wanting to be well informed, a marvelous cook. I'll never forget her lemon meringue pies and her short ribs of beef, her relatives favored her baked beans. Her husband, he just enjoyed it all, whatever.

Sarah and I had many talks about death and dying. In her life time she had two narrow escapes, one as a child when she was mysteriously saved from a poisoning. It seems two girls were given candy; they both ate the candy. The other girl died, and of course Sarah lived. There was a lot of talk among superstitious people. In those days, folks believed all kinds of bizarre things. Sarah was a very frightened little girl; this all left quite an impact on Sarah's life. People wondered how this girl was able to survive, as if she had some unknown power. As time went on, the people were able to put it in the back of their minds. Later in life, when Sarah's children were grown, she developed a cancer and was cured. I think there was always this search going on in Sarah's mind. One that I helped to satisfy. I spent her last three years telling her of my experiences. I used to read poems to her over the phone; she seemed to enjoy listening. Our friendship was constant.

Sarah's husband was ailing, in and out of the hospital. He was all she had to hold on to; what with the children grown and married, living in other towns. That was the time our friendship really blossomed. Her husband passed away quietly with a smile on his face(adorned in the white robe, a symbol of purity). That's the key, when the soul is clothed in a white robe, it is a pure soul. I saw her husband later, he was smiling that broad smile of his as if getting ready to tell one of his jokes, something he was well known for.

When my friend Sarah was confined to the hospital, I knew she would not get well. She pined so for her husband. With him gone there was nothing, children cannot take the place of a mate. She longed for the heaven world, (unconsciously that is). I was so glad I had spoken with her a few days before she made her transition. I was happy that I spent the last three years of her life preparing her for the lovely exit. She was not surprised when she made the transition, nor was she surprised when her husband was there waiting for her. Sarah came to me many times. She used to sit in my chair at night as if to just be there with me; to let me know all was well. She was always happy. Then one day she came to me to let me know she and her husband were to be born again together as twins, somewhere in France. It was my first experience of having someone inform me they were to be born again and the country they would be born in. Amazing isn't it. I somehow feel just as close to friends after they made the transition as I did before and maybe, I can even say more so. I just love them and maybe that's the key, although I see people I never knew in life. An example, I was reading the obituaries one day, I saw a picture of a man I never knew and immediately tuned into his transition. There he was in the heaven world happily playing an instrument. It was an instrument I was not familiar with but it came right into my consciousness that it was a lyre. I went to the dictionary to look up lyre and was surprised to see it was an ancient Greek instrument. So I went back to the obituary only to discover this man had a Greek name, offering me all the proof I needed. I can see anyone make the transition. I can literally see into the soul. What a gift I didn't know how I ever could have deserved this marvelous gift. I think the reason it was given to me was God knew I would not exploit it, never, never, never.

All I ever wanted in this world was to be of help wherever I am able. After all, God made an artist out of me to help my livelihood. Why should I not share the other wonders for free? I've always been grateful and always will be. You see it's not an ordinary thing. You know it isn't. Yes, it amazing, even though I constantly watch souls transiting from the earthly life to the after life, it never ceases to amaze me. How is this all possible to see these souls? Why it's as though I had a color television set in my head. Everything is so clear, more clear than life. I'm sure my book will get mixed reactions, after all it is an unusual gift to see with such clarity and to be able to recall at any given moment any situation with all its detail. I tell you to tap that Divine energy is a most marvelous experience and it's not just for me, it's for anyone who reaches the stage in their own evolution to awaken the Divine. You don't necessarily have to see into the heaven world as I do, but it will open something of an unusual nature. If you don't reach some sort of genius, you haven't reached that high state of consciousness; you haven't tapped the source, that special source that only comes from God.

Just this minute on television, they are talking about a very brave woman who passed away not long after burying her beloved husband under an unusual circumstance. His demise through a murder, yes he was murdered, she succumbed through the sickness of cancer. Only her family knew of her sickness. I'll say brave. When this lovely lady made the transition, she saw herself as a mermaid, a beautiful young mermaid swimming across the water until she came up on the other side. On the beach she met her husband, he was waiting for her with a white robe in his hand. She donned the robe, they embraced and commenced to walk to the woods. They then followed a trail leading up into the woods, they came to some steps. They ascended the steps which seemed never ending. Finally, at the top they came to a clearing and there was a settlement of Buddhist; they faded into the group. Strange isn't it, uncanny really, in some other or the previous life time they must have been Buddhist.

Imagine me writing about my experiences into this unknown land; this land so few are familiar with. They always say no one has ever come back to tell what the other side of life was all about. Not so, I can vouch for that. Yes, me a person who has always been plagued by fears. People speak of the souls that have gone on as ghost or spirits. Those words are scary; most people would be frightened if they saw someone deceased; not so with me. I over came my fears quickly and don't think for one minute it wasn't Divine intervention. How else could you overcome a lifetime of fearing the so called dead in two weeks. I say dead, but there is no such thing as dead. The souls are alive and doing well in their spiritual souls in the other world.

You know there has to be more, every denomination speaks of a special place. I hope that friends won't be alarmed to read that I have been there and I know. Remember we are coming into the age of miracles. Yes, miracles will be again. The proof will be given to mankind. The Divine knows all and is way ahead of us. The Divine knows that in this age a sign is required. It will be given, it will all be proven. Raise your consciousness up high, beyond the sky, then you will know the reason why. We live, we live, souls never die.

There are so many cases. Transitions all so different. I could go on and on, but I think I've whet your appetite enough; given you a good insight into what to expect when you make your own transition. Whether you believe or not is up to you. In the end when life is no more, you will see, you will believe. The transition we all have to make. Most cases are absolutely beautiful, for the others; angels are always waiting, waiting to assist as long as you don't resist. Believe it's all true. Thank you God for the knowledge, the insight, for the beautiful awakening.

PART II

As I share Transitions with my public, I would feel
remiss if I did not share some of my first poems.
These poems mark the very beginning of my path
toward a higher state, without knowing my soul was
transpiring efforts toward this divine manifestation
that now overwhelms and calms at the same time.
This treatise is only the beginning, there is so much
more to divulge.
My devotion is to the Divine source that brought me
this far. Nothing can stand in the way or mar. I give
it to you as it came to me. There'll be no blunder, on
with my wonder.

November 26, 1975 — It Started

November 26, 1975

God Is
God is mercy
God is light
Gentle bliss
Out of sight
Who can see God
Very few
A glow everywhere
With a gentle luminous hue
Discover God
You, you and you
Everywhere.

November 28, 1975

Love is a simple thing
A child's delight in early Spring
Love is remembering days gone by
Love is kindness, fulfillment
Love is everything
Love is a starlit sky
A moonlit night
A gentle breeze passing by
And a rainbow across the sky
Love is eternal
Love is happiness
Sweet sorrow
Love is pure
Love is a blessing
Love is grace
These things and many more
Love is.

Remembering

Autumn is almost over
The trees are bare
No trace of Summer anywhere
The purple martin, robin
And red wing black bird
Have all flown South
Leaving the sparrow, blue jay
And cardinals
Squirrels scurrying here and there
Gathering in the nuts
For the Winter's fare
Soon the snow will come
Deer fleeting across the meadow
How graceful
Autumn is almost over
But I shan't care
As she'll leave me remembering
Her special beauty
Defy Autumn if you dare.

To Discover Truth

My search for the truth is not in vain
I'm searching everywhere
I've read Steiner, Krishna and Massy
Studied the religions of the world
To question those wonderful masters
I would not dare
My search for truth must never end
For I truly care
Oh! Yes I know, I'll search within
Surely, truth will be there.

Beauty is everywhere
On a hillside, on the lake
In a babbling brook
And a quiet country nook
A water fall, a mountain tall
A soft summer breeze
The lovely colors of early Fall
Beauty is everywhere
You'll find beauty in the fluffy clouds
You'll find it at the shore
You'll find it in the valley
Beauty forever more
Did you ever look for beauty
In the stars so bright at night
Or in the moonlit evenings
Such beauty is sheer delight
Beauty, beauty everywhere.

Remember star light, star bright
First star I've seen tonight
Well, I wished upon a star last night
I wished and wished with all my might
That all the people of the world could
Unite
In true brotherhood
With a common bond of love
Understanding, peace, tranquillity
Sharing, caring, doing good
In true bonds of brotherhood
Star light, star bright
Maybe I won't get my wish tonight
But, if we tried with all our might
Someday we'd be beyond our plight
I wish, I wish, I wish tonight.

November 30, 1975
Morning Doves

As I gaze out of my window
At the morning dove
It fills my heart with gladness
Such a wonderful display of love
And to think, from a dove
They step aside while other birds eat
One after the other
Wouldn't it be wonderful if we humans
Had such consideration for our
Sister and brother
We can learn a lesson from the
Morning dove
Patience, tolerance and love.

Could I
Should I
Reveal my love
For all that surrounds me
The flowers, the animals
The birds and bees
The flowers scent the air
With a fragrance beyond compare
The animals protect our forest
Disturb them, I would not dare
The bees give us delicious honey
So sweet and clear
The flowers, the animals
The birds and bees
To me are so very dear
Accept this small expression
Of my love
For love that is truly real
Comes only from God above.

I believe in miracles
I believe in love
I believe in God
Sure as stars above
I believe in chivalry
Integrity, honor, sincerity
And such
I believe in all these things
Very, very much.

Sing a song of praise
Sing it loud and clear
About the creator
We love so dear
Sing a song of happiness
Filled with rhythm and zest
Sing a song with all your heart
Give your very best.

Wake up, wake up, tis morning
A new day is dawning
Get up, you sleepy head
Get up, get out of bed
Raise the window high
Breath in fresh air
Give out a sigh
Make today a special day
Spread good cheer
Be filled with mirth
A new day has given birth
Make others happy in some special way
And you'll be happy at the end of the day.

You can climb the highest mountain
You can swim from shore to shore
You can travel all around the world
It could be just a bore
But when you travel inwardly
To consciousness unbound
The treasures that await you
Few have ever found.

Oh! My look at here
We're at the dawning of a new year
What will it hold
What will it be
I say, down with strife
Confusion and blame
In seventy six, we don't need the same

I love you dear creator
Love you in the Fall
I love you in the Winter
Love you most of all
How can I express this feeling
This wonderful joy
I feel so exhilarated
Just overwhelmed with Thee
At this new development taking
Place in me
Is there a mission
What will you have me do
I'm at your disposal
With a sincerity that's true.

Full moon, stars shining bright
The awe and wonderment of the night

The universe, so vast and mysterious
Makes me feel both happy and delirious
Who can unlock her secrets
Surely, someday, somewhere
It will unfold
The greatest story ever told
So raise your consciousness up high
Unlock the secrets of the sky
Never was the need so great
For energies that are ours to take
Now, if we become ego bound
A Pandora's box will sure be found
So my advice to all youth
Is stick to the path that leads to truth.

We've traveled to the moon
Put satellites on Mars and Jupiter
Who knows where we'll travel
In the distant future
Or by what method we'll arrive
When this old world
Can no longer survive
Dare we think of such a day
We might even discover a new milky way
What's out there besides open space
Science get busy
It's running late
Your methods are way out of date
Conquer space.

December 2, 1975

A stranger knocked at my door one day
I wanted to say, go away
But then I thought
Who might he be
Someone bearing a message for me
He had a book tucked under his arm
Smiled and was filled with charm
I opened the door wider and let him in
He gave me even a bigger grin
He said he was spreading God's word
I said young man haven't you heard
All the Gods are within
Open your heart and let them in.

Doctors, doctors, hear our plea
We depend on you, don't you see
Even though we know you're not God
Some of your mistakes
Will put us in the sod
You're one hundred years
Behind in knowledge
Everything worthwhile
Is not learned in college
Doctors, doctors, what is wrong
We urge you to get back
Where you belong
In the spirituality of things
Praises to you we then will sing
Open up your hearts and minds
You'll receive knowledge of all kinds
Doctors, doctors, please
Expand your consciousness
Be at ease, help humanity
Be rid of disease.

December 4, 1975
Higher Consciousness

Relaxed
Waiting for sleep to come
Instead of sleep
Brilliant light
Boundless
Filling every corner of my existence
I marvel at the sight
Luminous shades of blue
Billowing forth one cloud after the other
Surrounded by emerald green
Flowing out into the where
Invaded by a beautiful copper orange
Here and now
I'm spellbound by this magnificent array
Of color
Interested
Then come with me into my fantastic
World of dreams in the awakened
Are you sure you have the courage
They're not ordinary dreams you know
They're real, fantastically so.

Behold a marvel in the darkness
A huge ball of orange brightness
Out in space against a midnight
Background
Bursting in sparks and glows
Of a million fragments
How out of the ordinary for me
Am I witnessing the bursting of an atom
I drift off to a heavenly sleep
It's five o'clock in the morning
A new day is dawning
I'm wide awake
Out there in the stratosphere
Above the clouds
Reminding me of a painted desert
Way out in the sky
Suddenly realizing I'm traveling to realms
Where man has never been before
Except in higher states of consciousness
Earth seems so far away
Will I make it back today.

It's now mid-afternoon
Finished up my morning tasks
Relaxed in my easy chair
My whole existence is filled
With glowing lights of color
I'm drifting off like a bird in the sky
To some far off place
I've never been before
Everything is so bright and colorful
More real than your existence
I stop
Yet do not recognize this beautiful land
I've traveled half way around the world
This way
Should I write a book about
My adventures into the unknown
But would you know how real
It is not just a story told
Of that I would not be so bold
There's more, there's more to be told.

The Divine Energy

From the very tip of my fingers
To the tips of my toes
Energy flowing with a tingling sensation
Surging it's way through my body
Culminating in my brain
Bursting forth with such dignity
Like it knows the path it has to travel
Preparing my body for the new birth
Sometimes escaping out of my eyes
Filling the atmosphere around me
With it's luminous luster
Heart pounding in my ear
Like the beat of a drum without rhythm
Blood pressure rising
The phenomena of rebirth if successful
Transcends the normal limits of the brain
This is a natural awakening of
The divine energy.

Silence

Did you ever stop to think of silence
There's no such thing as silence
When you're alone there is no silence
In your home, no silence
We may be very quiet
Yet there is no silence
Meditation is not complete silence
Explain the mystery of silence
The dictionary states, and I quote
" silence is refraining from speech
Making no sound"
Did you ever try making no speech
With real silence or no sound
The only true silence is when
You're steeped in contemplation
And reach a oneness
This is silence.

God's Promise

My rainbow I do give
In a cloud
God's promise
To all mankind
How beautiful it is
To feast your eyes
Upon this rainbow
Where every object
Gleams
Ecstacy and awe
At God's wonder
To witness this spectacle
How precious
How sweet
Glory be
To it's Creator.

It's time again to venture
Into my wonderland of dreams
In the awakened state
I tell you true
Until I reach my destination
I know not what to expect
But one thing sure
It always begins
With a brilliant hue of blue
That cannot be duplicated anywhere
It's true, it's true
Off I sail into the night
Beginning to unfold is a most
Unusual sight
A dramatic occurrence in the sky
Why! Fourth of July has long since
Gone by
And we don't have rockets on earth
To reach so high
What a beautiful display across the sky
Reds, blues, silvers and greens
All I can do is heave a sigh
At the marvelous sight that just went by.
It fills my being
With such a heavenly feeling
Why! Just a wee glimmer
 T'would leave the average person's
Head a reeling
Come venture inward
To those far distant shores
Please do try, you need not oars
Expand your consciousness
It's yours, it's yours
It's yours to behold.

December 23, 1975

I could write a sonnet
Put lots of frills upon it
But I'd rather get down
To the simple fact
Would you believe
Will you take heed
I urge you get ready
It's time to act
How much proof is needed
I deal in fact
The world is in shambles
We continue to gamble
This age of materialism has got to cease
We're in dire need of world wide peace
It won't be tolerated much longer
There is so much at stake
All this confusion makes my heart ache
Think of how this world can be
A paradise for you and me
I urge you all
Let's get together and live under one
Worldly roof
United forever and ever in peace.

Nature has provided
For all our needs
Yet we continue
To do wrong deeds
There's enough food
To feed all mankind
We can straighten out
This system
If we only tried
But we continue
Through life
With so much hatred and greed
Bringing on more
Pestilence and disease
If we'd but straighten up our minds
All these things will fall in line
And make this earth a pleasant place
For all inhabitants of the human race.

I can hardly stare
At the new fallen snow
Everything forms colors
For me you know
With the help
Of the sunbeams
I witness such beauty
Where ever I go
I wish there was some way
To you I could show
Because that's the only way
You'll really know.

December 23, 1975

Dear World
We're into the bicentennial year
Looking over the past
What did we gain
Has two hundred years
Gone down the drain
Filled with remorse
Littered with pain
It all seems so insane
We've had nothing but strife
One thing after the other
Look what we're doing to our brother
Are we trying to annihilate life
With power hungry games
And forbidden spice
Too much sex
And not enough rice
Pornographic movies and drugs to entice
Have we learned our lesson
Paid our price, evened the score
Let's close the book
And repeat no more
In seventy six
Let's love and adore.

There's another story to be told
Not a tale, a yarn or a story of old
T'is of a new happening, happening to me
And I wasn't sitting under a bodhi tree
I lay in my bed awaiting for sleep
And what do you know, I had a peep
Into my fantastic world of awareness
Colors in kaleidoscope all over the place
Intricate designs one could never trace
If I were an artist I would astound
Because of this work of beauty I've found
My wish is that I could take you in
But you have to find it for yourself
By looking within.

Row, row, row your boat
Gently down the stream
Merrily, merrily, merrily, merrily
Life is but a dream
Now who says so
Is this the dream
To watch babies scream from hunger
To see poverty worldwide
To watch young men go off to war
Thou shall not kill
Life is but a dream
I'd say a nightmare for some
To see the crime rate soar
Shall I tell you more
Our education system is on the rocks
Instead of scholars we're turning out
Blocks
Our food supply is being poisoned
With additives

Who needs them
Can we go back to the old way of life
Add a little more zest, a little more spice
Maybe things would turn out nice
With a little more of the old way of life.

In the cool of the evening
I'm bereaving
All the lost souls gone astray
God help them on this Winter's night
To understand their plight
Angels are waiting to assist
Break down the barriers
You must do this
To find the heaven world of bliss
There's nothing in lingering down below
Happiness is not there
You already know
Pay attention, follow the glow
Angels willing, able to show

It was early in the morning
Hardly a sound could be heard
I know this story might sound absurd
When all of a sudden
I was jetted out into darkness
I was a bit frightened, what have we here
I saw a wee light, in front was all clear
Next thing you know I was out of sight
I felt like a bird in flight
Way up here, I had a view
Better than any camera could take
How did all this happen
When I'm still wide awake
A thought of heaven bounced through
My head

Yet I knew I was still in my bed
How enchanting this experience
I tell you it's unbelievable
But it's most certainly true.

Wake up America

The world is in an awful mess
We're all being put through
A terrible test
Traveling through our country
Are lots of false prophets
We must get together and put a stop to it
With all kinds of programming
And brainwashing techniques
You'll blow your mind
The whole thing reeks
Why oh! why are people so gullible
Just tell them anything
They'll think you're so lovable
If the church were doing the job endowed
There wouldn't be followers
For the way out crowd
Living in communes
Eating food that's unhealthy
While their benefactors
Get extremely wealthy
Wake up America.

December 24, 1975

I feel a wee bit let down
There's no one around
To relate to
I'm not ego bound
I don't wish to hound
I just want someone to talk to
My cup runneth over with thoughts galore
I write them down
They just keep coming more and more
My thing is my own
A very different tune
If I express too much
You'll think I'm a loon
Have to admit I am somewhat of a goon
But, for now I beckon
Just allow me a second
I promise you when I get through
You'll be singing a different tune too.

What's this world all about
I'm simply ready to scream and shout
There's so much disorder and pain
I wonder what we hope to gain
Things just don't seem the same
When I look around I'm filled with shame.
Whether you know it or not
We're all to blame
I'll make a plan in my own special way
Maybe it won't save the day
But at least I will have made a start
To do my share and take my part.

Dear creator
Help us
On this very special day
That we don't allow ourselves
To be led astray
We know that you have all the answers
To end wars and cure cancers
Those of us who are seeking truth
Will gather together
Under one humble roof
We know that you'll guide us all the way
To teach others from day to day
That evolution must have it's way
There is so much to learn
Pray help us to discern
We're willing to sacrifice anything
We don't want to be martyrs
Or expect to live like a king
In our humble way
We hope and pray
That on this very special day
You will help us find the way
To save the world from being led astray.

He's got the whole world in His hand
Everything part of a universal plan
Let's get it together from land to land
And successfully carry out
The universal plan
And then we'll be part
Of a very happy clan
Working for the good hand in hand.

December 25, 1975

It was nineteen seventy six
The country was up to it's old tricks
The government was on rampage
Too much aggression for this age
We're nearing the time for brotherhood
The Aquarian age must be understood
We've been through many things before
Bombed out countries
Ill gotten wars
Is this what life is all about
Too little concern for our fellow man
Catch as catch can
There's a divine mission to fulfill
With a member from each nation
Guided by the hierarchy
Each will have a station
They'll unlock the secrets of the stars
Unleash new powers
From Jupiter and Mars
New found energy will be discovered
Just in time we will recover
From this upheaval
Lashed out against each other
Until that day if we may
Have one more chance to capture
The love for our brother.

December 27, 1975

In the evening
When the sun goes down
And it's semi- darkness
God lights appear
They're all around
Adding sparkle and light
To all they surround
By the window they glow
With a florescence so beautiful
Shimmering like rainbows
On the leaves and stems of the plants
With a transparency
Colors shining so bright
Giving sparkle and zest to the night
Why is this so special with me
I wonder if I could teach others to see
This beauty
Praise be to the creator
Whose gift of this special sight
Allows me to see the God light
Sparkling so heavenly through the night.

Maybe it's much too early in the year
But I thought I would consult you my dear
What course must I take
Please tell me in the morning
When I awake
I value your opinion with high esteem
Will I then awaken and find it just a dream
It's our secret
You know what I mean.

December 27, 1975

Sweet day dreams
Beautiful memories
Lingering in my mind
I relive those happy days
Those carefree ways
When we were young
We knew a different
Kind of love
Marriages
Were ordained from above
No matter how
We look at it today
Love is love
The same sweet way
Old sweet love
Beautiful memories
Linger on.

December 28, 1975

I raised my consciousness
And saw Buddha
Entering the body of Jesus
And the two became one.

January 1, 1976

What a beautiful day
To start the new year
The sky is so blue
The day bright
The air so clear
I feel a lovely calm
A sereneness
I've never felt before
For the new year
I promise
To develop those wonderful feelings
More and more
I shan't make false promises
Promises hard to keep
I'll just try to be reliable
Punctual
And love ever so deep
Do good to my neighbor
Pass judgement on no one
Take care of my love ones
Get all my work done
My friends I'll adore
No one will I deplore
I'll heed the call for help
Whenever I can
With lots of love and compassion
For my fellow man
Just a few things I'll practice my dear
Love to all and to all a good year.

January 2, 1976

My darling Creator
I love Thee
Love Thee with all my heart
So thankful for the understanding
You've given me
I'll never let anything or anyone
Tear us apart
I've learned so many lessons
Because You've granted me the sessions
Given me a new lease on life
Renewed hope
A brand new start
I would love to tell others
Of your wondrous love
And let them know You're everywhere
And stop searching above
You're able and willing
To answer every call
He's waiting
Please hurry
There's no time to stall
Our Creator wants a perfect world
Because He loves us all.

The snow has come
I love it
Children are thrilled by it
Laughter ringing
Throughout the neighborhood
Sleigh rides
Girls and boys dressed
In warm winter clothes
Hand knit hats and mittens
To protect them from the cold
Tis the season to be jolly I am told
Mountains and steep slopes
For those who crave excitement
And are brave and bold
Paradise for skiers
A wonderland for toboggan lovers
Professionals and beginners
Ice skaters frolicking around the pond
Landscapes touched
By nature's magic wand
The new found sport of snowmobiles
Young folks racing across the fields
Some taking spills
Some seeking thrills
Some sliding gracefully up and down hills
Winter magic I adore
Staying home would be a bore
Outside are thrills galore
Enjoy
The snow has come.

I love the country in the Summer
Adore it in the Fall
Just fascinated by it in the Springtime
But Winter is my favorite season of all
There's something magical about Winter
To me it brings a calm
Restfulness filled with peace
As I gaze at the Sun's reflections
It enchants me with a mystical glow
Colors dart about everywhere I gaze
More brilliant where there's ice and snow
Ice cycles like elongated diamonds
Give off a most brilliant hue
When kissed by the Sun and form prisms
Like you see on new fallen dew
None can compare with a Winter sunset
Sparkling across a lake
Or an early morning sunrise
As day is beginning to break
The snowflakes are so darling
Each with it's own design
The chill in the air is exhilarating
Mixed with the aroma of pine
Winter is truly wonderful
My favorite season of all
I hope you enjoy your Winter
Summer, Spring and Fall.

January 5, 1976

Day dreams
Night dreams
Wide awake dreams
Dreams so real
Dreams that appeal
Dreams of sorrow
Dreams about tomorrow
Dreams of love
Dreams that take place
In heaven above
Dreams that are fashioned
After our cares of the day
Dreams so very happy
We wish they'd stay
Dreams that are nightmares
Please go away
Dreams so vivid
You think them real
Dreams so ardently
Filled with zeal
Would you change your dream appeal
For what's true and sure
And positively real
I would.

Be joyful and gay
Give thanks for this day
Spread cheer along the way

Consider other people's needs
Perform a simple task
Do a pleasant deed
No need to wait for one to ask

Don't take advantage
Of a good thing
Accept favors graciously
Your heart will sing

Be content with whatever may
Let your inner voice lead the way

These are many things I could say
To help make this a better day
But I'll just say
Be joyful and gay.

Love thy neighbor
Don't hesitate to do a favor
You never know when
You'll have need
But if you're filled
With envy and greed
And can't live up
To God's creed
Well, suppose one day
You are in need
And no one will do you
A good deed
I'll tell you true
Your heart will ache
And you'll feel blue
If no one wants to bother
With you
Because you show no concern
Remember, respect
Has to be earned
A mighty lesson
You'll have learned
Be concerned
Love thy neighbor.

As I meditate on the Lord
I know I can't afford
To listen to what others say
About your coming
In a usual way
Folks don't seem to understand
How You'll come in a cloud
I understand perfectly
Feel so proud
To know the truth
Has set me free
And when my mission
On earth is through
Maybe I can be with You
Or maybe my mission
Might be
To teach others how to see
The beautiful rainbow
Bequeathed by Thee.

The Sun was shining
On this uneventful day
A little voice inside me
Seemed to say
Don't sit there a feeling blue
You can find plenty of work to do
Write a letter to a friend
Or bake a cake
It's a long time before day will end

I jumped up and busied myself
Took the dishes from the rack
And put them on the shelf
Later on I felt much better
Sat down and wrote a letter
Someone came in we had a chat
We talked about one thing and another
This and that
Next thing you know
Evening time had come
I thought about all the chores I'd done
Even wrote a poem
About events to come
This was rather a most eventful day
Never, never again will I say
I don't know what to do
And let a day waste away.

Events to come

I have a message
For the leaders of each nation
The time is at hand
Get together
Combine knowledge
Plan your station
With skillful management
A liaison if you please
With fact, finesse and ease
The end of this age has to be faced
Let's not end it with tension and disgrace
Whatever come what may
Together you can save the day
When the earth trembles and quakes
The seas churn and fires brake
These disasters will abound
Weird happenings near New York sound
Disruptions will center on
Japan and Greece
You'll wonder if those catastrophic
Conditions will ever cease
Remember we were forewarned
Some didn't believe
Some even scorned
There's still time to put things right
More togetherness, less strife
It's not so important for you and me
The children of the world deserve better
Do you agree
God help us.

A Letter To My Mom

Dear Mom
It fills my heart with gladness
Just to think of you
I miss you
And love to see you
Sometimes the thoughts
Make me feel so blue
I know I've always felt this way
But never could express
The love I have for you
Contains pure happiness
Accept this little token
Of my love
It will continue to flourish
Sure as stars above
My best to you each morning
Sincerely and such
Remember always
I love you very much
God love you.

Celestial lights
Beautiful sights
Descend to Earth
Giving birth
To new ideals
Hidden goals
Super conscious memory
To unfold
Of the paths
We once did follow
Paths of glory
Paths of old
There are missions
To fulfill
Here on Earth
When special souls are given birth.

Faith, hope charity
Expressed with precision
Distinction and clarity
Faith in the Creator
Who has brought us thus far
Faith that nothing can mar
The plan to be carried out
That will change this system
Completely about
Hope for the future
We preach
Destiny awaits us
We beseech
All will heed and rejoice
Spoken with a mighty voice
Wonders will never cease
Charity not material
Fashioned on true wisdom
Knowledge from the Deity
With contentment
When all is settled
Completion of the plan
We'll all live together
In a wonderland
To help carry out god's creed
Faith, hope and charity
Is all we need.

What am I going to do today
Something constructive something gay
Who knows what will come my way
Or shall I say
How can I help someone today
A phone call to a friend
An errand to attend
Maybe rest and read a book
Putter around the breakfast nook
I might just sew a dress
But then
The house is in an awful mess
I don't really care
I slave all year
Give my family the best
I'll do nothing, I don't care
But that's not what it's all about
To be plain lazy
I'm no lout
Where's the constructiveness
Where's the gaiety
Where are those wonderful
Thoughts of Deity
Get going
Your turmoil is showing
What are you going to do today
Something constructive, something gay.

No need to be lonely
No need to sit and pine
Look around you
Happiness is yours and mine
Visit a shut-in not able to get about
Spread cheer at the children's ward
Make them want to laugh and shout
There are so many troubled folks
Not able to function at all
Visit the local hospitals
You'll see them
Up and down the hall
Maybe then you won't feel so sorry
About your little plight
Do you know
Many people don't even have good sight
You have so much going for you
Yet you sit around and stew.

The way will be paved, direction shone
Plans by the Creator
Are never accomplished alone
Those necessary will enter your life
The work to be done
Will include more than one
He will light the way
We'll be taught at night
How to fashion the day
The invisible helpers will be at our side
Assisting as needed
Creating an atmosphere of pride
Ready and willing to always guide.

Some folks love to sit and complain
Everything for them must represent gain
How unfortunate I'd say
To sit and complain all day
I wonder what makes them that way.

Don't go around mad
Feeling bad
You make me sad
Come
I'll show you how to be glad
I'll tell you jokes
Written by my dad
He was a cad
But he could make
You feel glad
Don't be mad
If that doesn't help
I'll take you fishing
For shad
Or introduce you
To my brother Thad
He's a gay sort of lad
Who will really make you
Feel glad
I just can't stand
To see you
Go around mad.

Last night the moon
Was so beautiful and bright
As I gazed out my window
Into the night
The whole countryside
Was lit up with clear light
As far as the eye could see
Was quiet and peaceful
A tremendous delight for me
Wonderful thoughts
Went through my head
I was very tired
But too awe struck
To jump in bed
Don't know why the moon
Effects me so
May be the marvelous brilliance
Of it's glow
I'd love to write
A little story
About the moon
And all it's glory
Including all
The ancient potpourri
Moon, moon shining bright
May I always feast
In your delight.

I'm in love with love
The whole year round
Oceans and oceans
Of love abound
I'd love to send
A little your way
To help make this
A happy day
Thoughts are things
They say
That can reach
Way out
So I'll think in love
And spread it
All about
If only it could reach
Around the world
Bringing about
Joy and peace
I love
And love
And love
And love
And never ever cease.

Hear ye, hear ye
The time is approaching
Listen carefully as I'm coaching
Stand in line, it will be fine
And just in time
Everything is paced
Help for the race
About face
We're into the new
Revelations it's due
I'll be bringing good news to you
And you
This is not idle chatter
It really does matter
Forces not to scatter
Get on board the hallelujah train
Much, much to gain
Naught to feign.

ABOUT THE AUTHOR

Vivian Gaines Tanner Paxton, a native of Newport, R.I. and a long time resident of the Hudson Valley resides in Hyde Park, N. Y.. She is a cosmetologist, poet and author. The author is a self taught artist and operates the Paxton-Tanner Gallery with her husband, John. She is of a spiritual nature and aspires to bring out the divine within herself, without realizing the ultimate state, no thought of reaching anything special. A whole new world opened to her. This treatise is the beginning of the revelation of her experiences that chronicle her spiritual awakening.

> A reality beyond real
> Told with zest and zeal
> As she breaks the seal
> A mystical knowledge
> Old made new
> For all to view
> The reign of the Queen.